The Nature and Science of
LEAVES

Jane Burton and Kim Taylor

Gareth Stevens Publishing
MILWAUKEE

For a free color catalog describing Gareth Stevens Publishing's list of high-quality books and multimedia programs, call 1-800-542-2595 (USA) or 1-800-461-9120 (Canada). Gareth Stevens Publishing's Fax: (414) 225-0377. See our catalog, too, on the World Wide Web: http://gsinc.com

Library of Congress Cataloging-in-Publication Data

Burton, Jane.
The nature and science of leaves / by Jane Burton and Kim Taylor.
p. cm. -- (Exploring the science of nature)
Includes index.
Summary: Discusses different kinds of leaves, the forms and colors
they may have, and their functions.
ISBN 0-8368-1942-X (lib. bdg.)
1. Leaves--Juvenile literature. [1. Leaves.] I. Taylor, Kim.
II. Title. III. Series: Burton, Jane. Exploring the science of nature.
QK649.B88   1997
575.5'7--dc21   97-8478

First published in North America in 1997 by
Gareth Stevens Publishing
1555 North RiverCenter Drive, Suite 201
Milwaukee, Wisconsin 53212 USA

Printed in the United States of America

1 2 3 4 5 6 7 8 9 01 00 99 98 97

Contents

Words that appear in the glossary are printed in **boldface** type the first time they occur in the text.

The Life of a Leaf

It is dark in a forest because light from the Sun is blocked by trees. The leaves on the trees collect most of the Sun's light. Green leaves are a plant's food factory. Leaves produce food the plant needs for growing and making flowers, fruits, seeds, and new leaves. Energy in the form of light from the Sun is used by leaves to turn **carbon dioxide** and water into **oxygen** and **sugar**. This process is called **photosynthesis**. Green plants use sugar as a basic food.

Leaves come in many shapes and sizes, but nearly all leaves accomplish the same tasks. Most spread themselves out to capture maximum sunlight and use the sunlight to make food for the plant. As leaves age, they fall from the tree. Trees that lose their leaves in winter stop growing because their food factories "close" for the season.

Right: The leaves of many eucalyptus trees, found in Australia, do not spread out to catch maximum sunlight, but hang vertically. This keeps the leaves from burning in the strong Sun and dry air. But they still get the light they need for photosynthesis.

4

Each kind of plant has leaves that are unique in shape. Some leaves are short and round. Others are long and thin, like needles. Some are simple; others are compound. Compound leaves are made of many small leaflets arranged in rows or spread out like the fingers on your hand. Leaves may be smooth, curly, "hairy," or have sawlike edges or sharp points.

Opposite: Most leaves spread out to catch the Sun, so it is shady and dark on the forest floor. Grass and ferns can only grow in open spaces where sunlight reaches the ground.

Cotoneaster has a simple oval leaf, pointed at the tip.

Nettles have simple oval leaves that taper to a point, with sawtooth edges. The leaves are covered with hairs that sting.

Lawson cypress leaves are tiny overlapping scales that cover the branches.

The Norway maple has a simple leaf.

Blackberry leaves are compound with usually three to five leaflets.

Mountain ash leaves are compound with the leaflets arranged in rows on each side of the leaf stalk.

The scales are forced open.

The shoot lengthens.

Then, the pale, crinkly leaves unfold.

Sap pumps the soft, new leaves into shape.

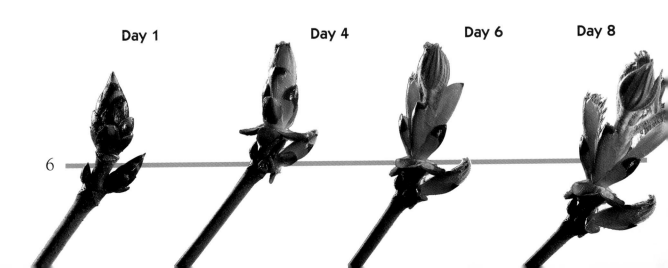

Day 1   **Day 4**   **Day 6**   **Day 8**

6

Growing Leaves

Over a million leaves can probably be found in a large tree. Many types of trees lose all their leaves in winter (or during the dry season). But when the weather improves, each of the trees becomes covered with **buds** containing tiny new leaves ready to burst open. The buds are covered by hard scales that protect the tightly folded leaves inside. In spring, the tree's **sap** starts to rise. Sap is made of water that is drawn up through tiny tubes in the trunk of the tree. The water then travels along the branches.

When the rising sap reaches the buds, the buds start to swell. The scales are forced apart. Then the sap pumps open the soft green stems and the bright crinkly leaves that have been held firmly inside the buds. The stems lengthen, and the new leaves and flowers unfold.

Opposite: Leaves burst from buds that grow on branches of trees. Inside the buds, tiny leaves are perfectly formed and folded tightly. When conditions are right inside and outside the buds, the buds swell and open.

Below: This bud of a horse chestnut burst open after three weeks of warm spring weather. At four weeks, the leaves spread fully.

Day 9   Day 12   Day 20

7

Leaves Need Water

Leaves need a large amount of water. Water flows up the stem of a plant as sap and enters the large and small **veins** in its leaves. The large veins are rigid. They keep the leaf from flopping over. The small veins fill in the spaces between the large veins. Besides bringing water to all the **cells** of the leaf, the veins stiffen the leaf to keep the wind from tearing it.

Leaves use some of their water for making food, but much of it is released into the air through thousands of tiny holes called **stomata**. As the leaves release **water vapor** through the stomata, the plant's roots draw water from the soil and pump it up the stem. A big tree draws several tons of water from the soil in order to open its leaves each spring.

Opposite: The light shines through this young oak leaf, clearly revealing its veins. The speckled bush cricket spends its life among the leaves because leaves keep the air moist and cool.

Above: The veins of this begonia leaf can be clearly seen. They support the leaf and bring water to it.

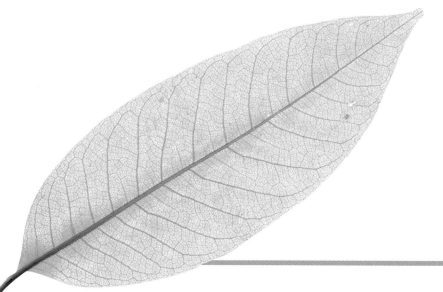

Left: When an old leaf falls to the ground, its softer parts rot away. Only a dry and delicate skeleton is left.

No Leaves, No Rain

Below: Cacti live in the dry desert regions of North and South America. Their stems store water and accomplish photosynthesis, just like leaves.

Most of the time, you cannot see the water that leaves release because it is in the form of vapor. But sometimes a plant (such as the water milfoil, *opposite*) draws up so much water during the night that the tips of its leaves are covered with water drops in the early morning. While the air is cool and damp, the drops do not **evaporate**. They glisten in the Sun. But as the air warms, the drops rapidly disappear.

Wherever there is an abundance of plants, the air is moist. This moist air makes rain. In places where people cut down the forest and destroy the natural plant cover, the land often turns to desert.

Only a few types of plants, such as the cactus, can survive in the desert. The leaves of cactus plants are sharp, dry spines that do not release water. The spines protect the plant from being eaten by animals.

How Leaves Breathe

Plants are able to "breathe" through their stomata. A medium-sized tree leaf, such as holly (*above*), may have more than 100,000 stomata on its underside. Stomata are so tiny they can only be seen with a **microscope**. Plants do not breathe in and out the way animals do. Air simply moves through the stomata.

All animals breathe in oxygen and breathe out carbon dioxide. Plants do the opposite. During the daytime, they breathe in carbon dioxide and

Below: Leaves cannot photosynthesize at night because there is no sunlight. The stomata in these quiver tree leaves in southern Africa close at night to prevent water from escaping.

release oxygen. At the same time, they also release water vapor. During the night or during very dry weather, stomata close into tiny slits, and the plant's breathing slows down.

All the oxygen in the air today has been made over millions of years by plants breathing. Our planet suffers when forests are completely destroyed. Destroying forests and burning the wood reduces the amount of oxygen and increases the amount of carbon dioxide in the atmosphere.

Above: Each leaf of this wayfaring bush has thousands of stomata on its underside. Throughout the day, the leaves use light to make sugar, and release oxygen into the air. The red berries turn black as they ripen.

Why Leaves Are Green

Most leaves are green because of the **chlorophyll** in their cells. Chlorophyll is a green **pigment** that absorbs energy from the Sun. This energy combines the water in the leaf with the carbon dioxide gas the leaf absorbs through its stomata. When carbon dioxide and water combine, the result is sugar and oxygen. Plants that do not receive sunlight cannot make chlorophyll. Their leaves are yellow, not green.

Plants also need **minerals** to build the millions of cells in each of their leaves. Minerals are in the water that plants draw up from the soil.

Opposite: The leaves on all the trees and other plants in this woodland spread out to catch light for photosynthesis. Plants on the ground can only grow where light shines through gaps in the trees.

Right: A chunk of dead bark fell off a tree onto this ground ivy. The stems of the ivy grew longer in the dark under the bark as they tried to reach the light. The ivy's leaves are yellow because they have no chlorophyll.

15

Flowers usually have brightly colored petals that show up clearly among the green leaves. But most flowers are not green. They do not photosynthesize. Their job is to make seeds. They attract butterflies and other insects that will carry **pollen** from one flower to another to **fertilize** them.

The wings of the green hairstreak butterfly look similar to honeysuckle leaves (*opposite*). But, unlike plants, the green color of the butterfly's wings does not come from chlorophyll, and the butterfly cannot make its own food by absorbing sunlight. No animal can do that — only green plants are able to make food from sunlight.

Right: The pink petals of this flowering, ivy-leafed geranium stand out clearly against the green leaves.

Special Leaves

Some leaves are so special that, besides catching sunlight to feed the plant, they actually catch insects. The tips of the leaves of the Venus's-fly-trap *(opposite)* are traps that snap shut if an insect touches the little hairs in the middle of the trap. When an insect is caught, it is digested by the plant and turned into plant food.

Bougainvillea plants *(above)* have somewhat dull little flowers with tiny petals. But brightly colored leaves surround the flowers. These leaves and those of the poinsettia *(below)* do not do a good job of photosynthesis but are very good at attracting insects.

Above: Mexican butterwort, like the Venus's-flytrap, lives in mineral-poor, boggy soil. Its leaves trap insects with tiny drops of sticky material located on the upper surfaces of the leaves. Minerals from the insects' bodies are used by the Mexican butterwort in the same way that minerals from the soil are used by other types of plants.

Leaves as Food for Animals

Animals depend on leaves not only for oxygen, but for food, as well. Most animals are plant-eaters, or **herbivores**. And most herbivores eat leaves. Some animals are meat-eaters, or **carnivores**. They eat the animals that have eaten leaves and other parts of plants.

The six-spot burnet moth caterpillar (*opposite*) feeds on a plant called birdsfoot trefoil. The green leaf being eaten has taken in the Sun's energy and changed it into **chemical energy**. The caterpillar eating the leaf is using this chemical energy to grow.

When a bird eats a caterpillar, the energy in the caterpillar changes into the bird's energy. This energy originally came from leaves eaten by the caterpillar.

Right: A bird called a blue tit carries a caterpillar back to its nest to feed its young.

21

Below: Sweet potato plants die back in dry weather, leaving underground **tubers** full of starch and sugar made by the leaves. The tubers are rich food for pigs, monkeys, and other animals that dig. If left uneaten, the tubers sprout again in spring.

Big animals as well as small animals eat leaves. Many kinds of large herbivores — antelope, deer, cattle, giraffes, and even gorillas — get all or most of their food from leaves.

Sugar made in leaves travels in the form of sap to other parts of the plant. This is why the sap of many plants tastes sweet. The sugar that people add to food is the crystallized sap of sugarcane or sugar beet plants.

Of course, plants do not just make sugar — this is only the first stage. From sugar, plants make **starch** and other materials. Some plants, such as potatoes, build stores of starch in their roots. The part of the potato that is eaten is its stored energy. Other plants, such as cabbage, store food in their stalks. These roots and stalks provide food for many animals, as well as people.

Right: A cabbage is a giant bud. The leaves pack tightly around each other and around the central stalk. Over winter, cabbage plants store energy in their stems. Rabbits gnaw these stems during the cold months when other food is scarce.

The countless leaves on this tree use sunlight, water, and carbon dioxide to make food. A giraffe browses among the higher branches and has some of the leaves for a meal.

Changing Colors

Below: The liquid-ambar, or sweet gum, leaf looks like a maple leaf. This tree grows in North America and has been planted in many other countries. Its leaves turn bright colors in autumn as the green chlorophyll in them breaks down.

In autumn, leaves change color. The leaves of many trees and other plants die in a blaze of color. The chlorophyll pigment in them breaks down, and their green color fades. The leaves turn red, orange, and yellow, like these blackberry leaves (*opposite*). The bright colors were in the leaves all along but were hidden by the green chlorophyll. The red, orange, and yellow pigments protect the leaves by blocking the harmful **ultraviolet** rays in sunlight. The colors show themselves when the remaining energy from the chlorophyll flows out of the leaf cells back into the plant.

There is very little food left in yellow or brown leaves that have fallen, so animals seldom eat them.

Above: As autumn approaches, a touch of red appears in a sweet gum leaf.

Right: The green chlorophyll in this leaf is beginning to drain back into the tree, revealing the red pigment.

Below: At this stage, all the energy from the chlorophyll has flowed back into the tree, leaving only red and yellow pigments.

Below: As the leaf dies, only the yellow pigment is left, and the leaf falls. It takes with it very little of the tree's energy.

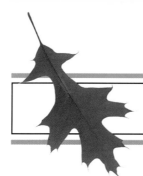

Falling Leaves

In most parts of the world, there are certain times of the year when leaves cannot do their work. In hot countries, trees shed their leaves during the dry season because of lack of water. In many other countries, leaves fall in autumn in a blaze of magnificent color because there is too little sunlight for food production.

Trees that lose all their leaves in a season, such as sweet chestnut, birch, maple, and oak, are **deciduous** trees. Before a leaf falls, a layer of cork grows between the leaf stalk and the branch so that the bare branch is protected.

Below: Sweet chestnut trees are deciduous and lose their leaves in autumn. The brown leaves and the chestnuts build up in layers of **leaf litter** beneath the trees. The fallen materials provide homes and food for small animals, and minerals for plants.

Left: The Joshua tree is actually a shrub and does not have the hard, woody trunk that a tree has. It is an evergreen, with sharply toothed leaves only at the tips of its branches. As the new leaves unfold from the top, the older leaves beneath them turn brown and fall.

Below: Scots pine is an evergreen tree with leaves shaped like needles. As they age, pine needles turn brown and fall off the tree at all times of the year. But there are always plenty of new green needles to take their place. The tree is never bare.

Most fir trees and some other types of trees have leaves throughout the year. These trees are **evergreens**. The leaves of evergreens fall when they reach a ripe, old age. But they do not fall all at the same time, and the trees are never bare.

Fallen leaves form leaf litter that helps keep the soil from freezing or drying out. It also provides homes and food for millions of small animals. Minerals from rotted leaf litter soak into the soil and feed the next crop of plants in the spring — when the cycle begins again.

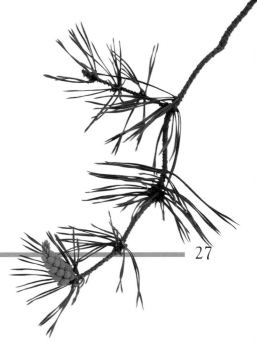

Activities:

Discovering Leaves

When you are in the countryside or in a city park, take a close look at the leaves you see. Even in winter, there are always evergreen trees with leaves. There are also dead leaves on the ground that you can observe. Each kind of tree or plant has its own particular shape of leaf. Leaf textures, or their "feel," also vary.

Plants that grow for one season only are called annuals. They often have soft, delicate leaves. The plants completely die in winter. In contrast, evergreen trees have tough, shiny leaves that can withstand the cold and winter winds. They survive winter and emerge healthy in the spring.

Making a Leaf Collection

To make a leaf collection, get a scrapbook or loose-leaf binder, sheets of newspaper, and some clear tape. Then collect twenty to thirty leaves to start. Do not pick leaves from small plants that have only a few leaves — the plant may wither and die.

Large trees, on the other hand, will not be harmed by losing a few of their leaves.

Select the leaves carefully, taking four or five from each kind of tree or other type of plant. Make sure you pick the whole leaf including its stalk. Some plants have leaves that vary quite a bit on the same plant, and you may need to gather ten or more leaves from the same plant to show all the different shapes. As you gather the leaves, try to think of the size of the pages in your scrapbook or binder. You are going to arrange all the leaves from one kind of plant onto its own page.

It is important to know the name of each plant from which you collect leaves. Identify the leaves you have chosen by consulting a plant guide, or ask someone to help you identify them. Make a note of both the common name of each plant (and any local variations you can find) and its more formal, scientific name.

Below: Leaves of many different types of trees and other plants can be found in a single area.

Pressing the Leaves

The leaves you gather will need to be pressed before they can be arranged on the pages of your scrapbook or binder. A plant press (*pictured*) is best for this. It consists of two wooden boards fastened together with wing nuts at the corners. If you don't have a press, flatten your leaves under something heavy, such as a large pile of books or a cement block.

To press the leaves, arrange them between layers of newspaper. Then put the completed layers in the plant press or under the books or cement block. Moisture in the leaves will gradually soak into the paper until the leaves become stiff and dry. This takes a week or two.

It is not necessary to collect only green leaves. Dead leaves can also be pressed. If you are lucky, you may find "skeleton" leaves (*see page 9*). These will give added interest to the pages of your collection.

When the leaves are dry, arrange those from each kind of plant on its own page. When you are satisfied with the arrangements, tape the leaves down as shown. Consult a plant guide, and write the common and scientific name of the plant on each page. You may want to include the date and the place where each type of leaf was found.

Leaf Rubbings

Another way of collecting leaf shapes is to make leaf rubbings. Find a firm leaf with strong veins. Lay it upside-down on a table under a sheet of thin, white paper. Rub a very soft pencil or a crayon over the paper, and watch the leaf's shape begin to appear. Cut out the drawing, and place it in your book as if it were an actual leaf. Increase your leaf collection year by year as you come across new types of plants. By adding leaves from different locations and climate zones, you can build a realistic picture of the world's plants — just like a professional botanist.

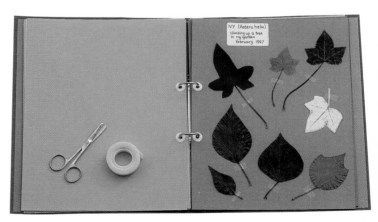

Glossary

bud: a swelling on a plant stem that contains new leaves or flowers.

carbon dioxide: a gas that is a combination of carbon and oxygen.

carnivore: an animal or plant that eats animals; a meat-eater. The plants that eat animals include bladderworts, butterworts, carnivorous mushrooms, pitcher plants, sundews, and Venus's-flytraps.

cells: the microscopic building blocks of plant and animal bodies.

chemical energy: the energy associated with the formation and breaking down of chemical bonds.

chlorophyll: the pigment that makes plants green. It is an essential part of photosynthesis.

deciduous: plants that lose all their leaves during one season of the year.

evaporate: to change from a liquid into a vapor.

evergreen: a plant that has leaves throughout the year.

fertilize: in the plant world, to cause a male cell to join with a female cell so that seeds form.

herbivore: an animal that eats only vegetation; a plant-eater.

leaf litter: the layer of dead leaves that forms beneath plants.

microscope: a scientific instrument that magnifies tiny objects to make them visible to the human eye.

mineral: a simple chemical found in the soil.

oxygen: a gas, essential for life, that forms about one-fifth of the air.

photosynthesis: a process by which plants use energy from the Sun to make food.

pigment: a substance that produces color in objects.

pollen: grains, usually yellow, in a flower that fertilize the female part of the flower.

sap: the watery liquid that contains nourishment for plants.

starch: a food material, closely related to sugar, that is stored in plants.

stomata: tiny holes in the leaves and stems of plants that are used by the plants for "breathing."

sugar: in the plant world, a sweet substance used by plants to store energy.

tuber: a swelling in the root system of some plants, where food is stored. An example of a tuber is the potato.

ultraviolet: a form of light energy from the Sun that is invisible to the human eye. Certain animals can see ultraviolet light.

veins: tiny tubes or bundles of tubes that support leaves and take water to them.

water vapor: water in the air in the form of a gas.

Plants and Animals

The common names of plants and animals vary from language to language. But plants and animals also have scientific names, based on Greek or Latin words, that are the same the world over. Each plant and animal has two scientific names. The first name is called the genus. It starts with a capital letter. The second name is the species name. It starts with a small letter.

birdsfoot trefoil (*Lotus corniculatus*) — Europe 20-21

blackberry, or bramble (*Rubus fruticosus*) — Europe; introduced worldwide 5

giraffe (*Giraffa camelopardalis*) — Africa 23

green hairstreak butterfly (*Collophrys rubi*) — western Europe, Russia, Asia Minor to Siberia 16-17

honeysuckle (*Lonicera periclymenum*) — Europe, North America 16-17

horse chestnut (*Aesculus hippocastanum*) — northern Greece and Albania; planted in Europe, North America 6-7, 26

ivy-leafed geranium (*Pelargonium peltatum*) — Europe, Asia, North America 16

jarrah (*Eucalyptus marginata*) — Western Australia 4

Joshua tree (*Yucca brevifolia*) — southern North America 27

Mexican butterwort (*Pinguicula caudata*) — Mexico; worldwide houseplant 19

mountain ash (*Sorbus aucuparia*) — Europe, northern Africa; North America 5

pedunculate oak (*Quercus robur*) — Europe, Russia, southwestern Asia, northern Africa 8-9

poinsettia (*Euphorbia pulcherrima*) — Mexico; worldwide houseplant 19

quiver tree (*Aloe dichotoma*) — southern Africa 12

six-spot burnet moth caterpillar (*Zygaena filipendulae*) — Europe 20

speckled bush cricket (*Leptophyes punctatissima*) — western, southern, and central Europe 8-9

Venus's-flytrap (*Dionaea muscipula*) — Carolina coast of North America; grown as houseplant elsewhere 18-19

wayfaring bush (*Viburnum lantana*) — Europe 13

whorled water milfoil (*Myriophyllum verticillatum*) — Europe 10-11

Books to Read

Bloodthirsty Plants (series). Victor Gentle (Gareth Stevens)

Eco-Journey (series). Behm and Bonar (Gareth Stevens)

A First Look at Leaves. Millicent Selsam (Walker)

It Could Still Be a Leaf. Allan Fowler (Childrens Press)

Looking at Plants. David Suzuki (John Wiley)

The Plant Cycle. Nina Morgan (Thomson Learning)

Plant and Flower. David Burnie (Knopf)

Tree. David Burnie (Knopf)

Trees and Leaves. Rosie Harlow (Warwick Press)

Videos and Web Sites

Videos

Deciduous Forest. (Coronet)
I Like Trees. (Video Dimensions)
Learning About Leaves. (Encyclopædia
    Britannica Educational Corporation)
Photosynthesis. (Encyclopædia Britannica
    Educational Corporation)
Photosynthesis. (Phoenix/BFA)
Plants Make Food. (Churchill Media)

Web Sites

www.whitemtn.org/autumn.html
www.learner.org:80/content/k12/jnorth/
    www/critters/leaf/825363593.html
www.dnet.net80/~cherokee/5th-grade/
    science.html
pc65.frontier.osrhe.edu:80/ns/science/
    keyword/bphoto.htm
www.discovery.com

Index